IMAGES
of America

DENVER'S PARK HILL
NEIGHBORHOOD

IMAGES
of America

DENVER'S PARK HILL
NEIGHBORHOOD

Rebecca C. Dorward

ARCADIA
PUBLISHING

Copyright © 2010 by Rebecca C. Dorward
ISBN 978-1-5316-5322-4

Published by Arcadia Publishing
Charleston, South Carolina

Library of Congress Control Number: 2009941017

For all general information contact Arcadia Publishing at:
Telephone 843-853-2070
Fax 843-853-0044
E-mail sales@arcadiapublishing.com
For customer service and orders:
Toll-Free 1-888-313-2665

Visit us on the Internet at www.arcadiapublishing.com

Again, as always, for my son

CONTENTS

ACKNOWLEDGMENTS

Whenever an author undertakes a book-length project, she must remember to thank many people and organizations. These include the Greater Park Hill Community (GPHC), Colorado Historical Society historians Heather Peterson and Chris Geddes, and historian and mentor Tom Noel. Personal thanks go to the late Dale Heckendorn for his assistance during my research for the Park Hill National Register Historic District. Thanks also go to Shawn Snow for his original inspiration, to GPHC director Greg Rasheed, to Park Hill residents Ed Kahn and Art and Carla Branscombe for sharing their experiences, to Arthur Rosenblum and Joan Wallach from the *Greater Park Hill News*, to Denver City Council member Marcia Johnson, to the Denver Public Library Western History Collection, to the University of Denver Penrose Library Special Archives, to the Stapleton Foundation, to the National Basketball Association's Denver Nuggets, to Marilyn Chang of the Wings over the Rockies Museum, to Kenton Forrest of the Colorado Railroad Museum, and last, but not least, to Jerry Roberts, Scott Davis, and Devon Weston of Arcadia Publishing for their expertise and patience.

INTRODUCTION

The primitive mining town of Denver, Colorado, was less than 15 years old when a few forward-thinking businessmen decided to speculate on new land developments. Caspar R. Hartman took the first step in 1871 when he purchased and platted Hartman's Addition. Several other real estate speculators followed his lead, buying and platting barren land: Downington in 1886, More's Park Heights in 1888, Strayers Park Heights in 1888, Park Hill Heights in 1888, and the Chamberlin Winnes Addition in 1889.

The name Park Hill originated with German immigrant Baron Allois Gullaume Eugene A. Von Winckler, who purchased a large 32-block tract of land north of Hartman's and platted it in 1887. Baron Von Winckler was an associate of Baron Manfred von Richtofen, who platted the Montclair Addition nearby in 1885. Baron Von Winckler constructed only two houses in the new addition, one for himself and an adjacent house for Walter C. Cox, who operated a dog pound. These houses were located approximately at East Twenty-second Avenue and Dahlia Street.

The year 1893 proved to be a bad one for Colorado and the entire nation. It was the year of the silver crash and a depression. Previously, Colorado silver mines had produced about 60 percent of the country's silver, but due to complicated factors involving a change to the gold standard, silver quickly lost its value. Silver mines closed, and men were put out of work. Many banks were forced to close. Denver residents lost their savings, and the economy turned sour.

So many unemployed men flocked to Denver that a tent city grew up along the South Platte River. The chamber of commerce provided money for the homeless to build flat boats, hoping the men would sail away down the Platte River and not come back to Denver. The goal was to march on Washington, D.C. to demand relief. Those who did not float down the Platte River boarded eastbound trains, sometimes for free. The political situation across the country became complicated due to the depression, and the economy did not recover for years. Despite the downturn, in 1893, the Cook's Horsecar Line began service along Thirty-fourth Avenue, along with the Park Railway Company, which had been operating since 1888, to provide transportation to the existing residents in the area. The assessor records are clear in showing a drop in building permits for that time, and the bad economy from 1893 to about 1900 was likely a major cause of the slow land sales in Park Hill.

The Park Hill Addition was sold in 1900 to a group of eastern land speculators who opened it up to development. Speculators and investors began buying lots in nearly every block of Park Hill and the adjacent additions. In many cases, the corners of the streets were the last to be sold, since many investors considered the interiors of the blocks as the more desirable lots. The price of a single lot varied from $150 in 1901 to about $300 in 1909, but location seemed to also increase the price. A two-lot parcel could be purchased for $300 to $500, an amount many local residents could find in savings accounts or cookie jars, and the solidity of investing in land appealed to those who distrusted mere paper stocks, such as in mining share certificates. In fact, the list of small land speculators who gobbled up the lots in Park Hill is unexpectedly long. A great many buyers appeared to be average Denver residents, not well known or particularly well-off, simply middle class workers and heads of families. Surprisingly, many lot purchasers were female—wives, daughters, or other relations. Of course, wealthy Denverites such as David Moffat, the J. S. Browns, the Iliffs, the Temple Buells, and others also bought Park Hill lots.

The first residences constructed there were architect-designed upper-class residences using several lots with alleyways, and these were located near Montview Boulevard. As time went on, builders began constructing houses on speculation, many from the Sears or Wards catalogs. The styles prevalent in Park Hill included the late Victorian, "Denver Square," Colonial Revival, Tudor Revival, and the popular bungalow. Remarkably, most of these homes still exist, with few alterations.

As the Baron's Park Hill began to sell, so did the neighboring areas. Much of the eventual success of these additions was due to the creation of public transportation services in the days before automobiles were affordable—first horsecars, then electric trolleys, then cable cars.

In 1924, Lowry Field welcomed all airplanes to its new Park Hill airport at Thirty-eighth Avenue and Dahlia Street. Charles Lindbergh landed his famous *Spirit of St. Louis* transcontinental airplane here in 1927, shortly after flying across the Atlantic Ocean. A parade down Colorado Boulevard celebrated his success. A year later, Amelia Earhart also landed here.

Adjacent to Park Hill, in 1929, Denver's first municipal airport opened. Charles Lindbergh and Amelia Earhart both landed there during the opening celebrations. In 1944, the name was changed to the Stapleton Airfield to honor Denver mayor Benjamin Stapleton, and in 1968, it became Stapleton International Airport. In 1995, Stapleton International Airport was officially closed as the new state-of-the-art Denver International Airport opened northeast of the metro area. The Stapleton area has been redeveloped into 21st-century residential living, offering new styles of housing, schools, and parks.

In the post–World War II housing shortage, Park Hill became the site of important struggles for integration in the United States. In 1949, the U.S. Supreme Court ruled that housing restrictions were unenforceable. Colorado improved its antidiscrimination and fair housing laws, and African Americans began to move to Park Hill. While initially Park Hill suffered from "white flight" anger and resentment, much like other parts of the country, a core group of residents and church officials attempted to solve the problems, keep white families in Park Hill, maintain single-family zoning, and welcome all new residents into Park Hill without regard to race.

A lawsuit against the Denver School Board went all the way to the U.S. Supreme Court, which ruled, in 1973, that the Denver Public School system must institute forced busing in several Park Hill schools and in other schools in the Denver Public School System. The case brought national attention to the Park Hill neighborhood. Denver neighborhoods as a whole did not escape the civil unrest that followed, but Park Hill residents fostered a willingness to have voluntary, as well as mandatory, school busing. Eventually Park Hill became a model for successful integration around the country.

The Greater Park Hill Community (GPHC) is a nonprofit neighborhood organization that formed as an outgrowth of the Park Hill Action Committee of the 1960s. The GPHC is staffed largely by volunteers and serves as a liaison between local residents and businesses and the City and County of Denver. The GPHC operates a food bank and thrift shop, and publishes a monthly newspaper, the *Greater Park Hill News*, which is distributed free to residents of Park Hill's administrative neighborhoods and nearby businesses.

In 1964, Dr. Martin Luther King Jr. gave several speeches in the Denver area, including a speech at the Macedonia Baptist Church on East Thirty-second Avenue and another at the Montview Boulevard Presbyterian Church. The citizens of Park Hill embraced his words and his attention to their neighborhood. Years later, in 1980, the name of Thirty-second Avenue was officially changed to Martin Luther King Jr. Boulevard from Downing Street to the west entrance of Stapleton International Airport.

Star professional basketball player Chauncey Billups was born and raised in Park Hill. While attending George Washington High School from 1991 to 1995, he became the state's most recognized athlete. Billups attended the University of Colorado, where he was named to the Big 12 Conference First Team and the *Basketball Times* All-American First Team. Drafted third overall in the 1997 NBA draft by the Boston Celtics, Billups was traded several times, achieving stardom with the Detroit Pistons. In 2008, Billups was traded to the Denver Nuggets, where he remains a star player. Other famous Park Hill residents include football player Mike Bell and Denver mayor John Hickenlooper.

Early in 2004, the 32 blocks of the original Park Hill subdivision gained recognition as a national and state historic district. This district is historically significant as one of the original exclusively residential areas near Denver, one of the first streetcar suburbs, and for its continuous record of architectural styles dating from approximately 1895 to 1941. Few alterations have occurred during the past century. The streets and houses are mostly the originals. Some houses have been remodeled, and an unfortunate few have been demolished, but for the most part, what is seen in Park Hill is the original.

At the end of 2008, the American Planning Association named the neighborhood of Park Hill one of the "Top 10 Best Places to Live" for its beautiful architecture and history. Perhaps the most important reason for this designation is the people of Park Hill, comprising every economic and educational sector, and the active neighborhood association. As Denver celebrates its 150th anniversary and the Park Hill neighborhood its 110th anniversary, it is truly an honor to bring to light the historic neighborhood of Park Hill.

One

THE BARON'S BACKYARD

The Park Hill addition, platted in 1887 by Baron Allois Gullaume Eugene A. Von Winckler, gave its name to the entire suburb of Park Hill. For 11 years, Baron Von Winckler tried unsuccessfully to bring residential development to this area. It was not until after his death in 1898 that this land became of real interest to developers. The name Park Hill is a misnomer, and "hill" is a relative term. The lands that comprise Park Hill are actually flat, with streets laid out in a north-south grid. The term "hill' derives from the height of the area relative to downtown Denver, which sits in a valley. The first Park Hill addition was Hartman's Addition, platted by Caspar R. Hartman in 1871. The land was miles away from Denver, and no one was interested in building homes there for many years. The Park Hill Syndicate purchased a large part of Park Hill and designated several restrictions. For example, every house had to be built on at least two lots and be set back 40 feet from the street. Row houses, apartments, churches, and stores were not allowed. Even the selling prices were designated. The syndicate controlled the size of houses by stating they must be built for at least $5,000 along Mont View Boulevard (original spelling) and $3,000 elsewhere. Corner houses located on Montview Boulevard had to cost at least $6,500, and $4,000 if built south of Twenty-third Avenue. Houses north of Twenty-third Avenue had to cost $3,000. In 1903, the City of Denver annexed the Park Hill addition, and the building restrictions were officially lifted. However, various neighborhood groups, such as the Park Hill Brotherhood and the Park Hill Improvement Association, encouraged the unofficial use of restrictions.

Denver of the 1880s was already a built-up commercial marketplace, which this view along Larimer Street suggests. Gaslights, electric lights, telephones, and public transportation were all features of the modern American city and were available in the city of Denver. (*Denver Municipal Facts,* 1909, Denver Public Library, Western History Department.)

A *Denver Times* article dated October 22, 1899, suggested, "There will be a big building boom in that large tract of unimproved property east of City Park next spring. The old estate where Eugene A. Von Winkler, the eccentric so-called 'German baron,' held undisputed sway until his death, some years ago, will be transformed into a small residences settlement, and the prairie dog and his associates, the owl and the rattler, will be robbed of their heritage." In 1909, Montview Boulevard in Park Hill shows a vacant, graded dirt street. This map below shows the location of the various additions in Park Hill. What is remarkable is that these additions were nothing more than wooden stakes on the natural windswept prairie, but the speculators were hopeful for the future. (Above, *Denver Municipal Facts,* 1909; below, *Denver Times,* 1901, Denver Public Library, Western History Department.)

Speculators Baron Von Winckler, Caspar R. Hartman, Jacob M. Downing, John Cook Jr., and Zophar W. More did not find many people rushing to buy their lots; however, a few old Victorian houses were constructed here and there. This advertisement shows a typical small Victorian house similar to those built on Thirty-fifth Avenue and Albion Street in the 1890s. (*Yesterday's Home*, Denver Public Library, Western History Collection.)

This Queen Anne–style Victorian was completed by 1892 on Thirty-fifth Avenue and Albion Street. The subdivision drilled a single well, and water was stored in a nearby water tank. Kerosene lamps provided light. In 1893, the Cook's railway line provided horsecar service along Thirty-fifth Avenue. A man named Jay A. Robinson was the first owner. The Robinsons did not have electricity or gas, only well water and a coal-burning fireplace for heat. Today this house, listed on the National Register of Historic Places, is a restaurant known as Kate's Restaurant on Thirty-fifth Avenue. (Rebecca Dorward Collection.)

Denverites, like Americans everywhere, enjoyed the parade to church on Easter Sunday. This photograph above shows a group walking to the downtown Trinity Methodist Church. The Park Hill area did not have any churches until 1910. (*Denver Municipal Facts*, 1909, Denver Public Library, Western History Department.)

Baron Von Winckler built a racetrack on his addition to showcase European jockeys and horses and to bring in money to the Park Hill area. A couple of years later, the City of Denver built a similar racetrack close to the first track, on Twenty-third Avenue and Colorado Boulevard. The City Park track proved more popular, and the Baron's track folded. The photograph shows the City Park racetrack with spectators watching in the distance. (*Denver Municipal Facts*, 1911, Denver Public Library, Western History Department.)

16

Baron Von Winckler had been a military man and was interested in assisting preparations for the war against Spain in 1898. He donated some of his land to the Colorado National Guard for training purposes. It became known as Camp Alva Adams. Young men from all around the state came there to enlist, drawn by the excitement of patriotism and travel to foreign lands. The military was reorganized as the First Colorado Infantry, led by Denverite Brig. Gen. Irving Hale. Daily life was primitive and centered on training, with drills several times a day. The soldiers slept in round Sibley tents, 16 to a tent. Often, a dress parade in the evenings brought out local residents and newspaper reporters to watch. The photograph above shows the same land today, now the Park Hill Golf Course. Below, in 1898, new recruits at Camp Alva Adams try to make sense of the uniforms they have been issued. (Above, Rebecca Dorward Collection; below, *Denver Municipal Facts*, 1910, Denver Public Library, Western History Department.)

In May 1898, the Colorado National Guard was mustered into federal service. In a public ceremony, Gov. Alva Adams handed every soldier four silver dollars as payment for state service. The guard paraded through downtown Denver and a few days later left town with a public farewell at the train station. About 1,100 Colorado soldiers were sent to the Philippines, not to Cuba as they had expected. In spite of that, and despite their outdated rifles and wool uniforms, the Colorado National Guard proved a successful fighting unit. Colorado troops raised the first American flag over the Philippines and later fought successfully against the Philippine insurrection. This parade served as a homecoming after the troops returned to Denver on September 14, 1899. (*Denver Municipal Facts*, 1911, Denver Public Library, Western History Department.)

On June 21, 1898, Baron Von Winckler committed suicide. His land was sold in late 1899 to an eastern syndicate consisting of businessmen David Gamble, of Proctor and Gamble; Earl Cranston; George Hamilton; and Robert T. Miller. The proceeds were sent to relatives in Germany. A ground-breaking ceremony took place in Park Hill around 1901 with Senator Elmer Merritt, a real estate investor, posing for the camera with a shovel of dirt. Lot lines are visible. A nearby sign stated, "Park Hill, This Property Will Be Sold on Easy Terms with Building Restrictions, Modern Houses for Sale." Progress was quickly made constructing streets, laying sewers and curbs, and planting trees. A few new houses were constructed for those adventurous families willing to live far from the comforts of Denver. (Above, *Denver Times*, October 22, 1899; below, *Denver Municipal Facts*, 1910, Denver Public Library, Western History Department.)

Speculators promoted Montview Boulevard heavily, but with few options for transportation into downtown Denver, only wealthy car owners could afford to live here. According to the *Denver Times*, dated January 14, 1902, "The Park Hill syndicate has sold eight lots on the corner of Montview boulevard . . . to Mr. W.R. Daniels, a Chicago capitalist . . . for $3,200, or $400 a lot. . . . Mr. Daniels' fine new house will be historic. It will be the starter of what can easily be made Denver's finest residence boulevard and most charming drive." In the fashion of the day, the land itself was titled in Margaret M. Daniels's name. (Above, *Denver Municipal Facts*, 1910, Denver Public Library, Western History Department; below, Rebecca Dorward Collection.)

Three architect-designed residences were constructed on Albion Street before 1909 and have 20th-century elements, such as low-pitched hip roofs and horizontal brickwork similar to the early designs of Frank Lloyd Wright. Above left is the Fisher and Huntington house, designed for Dr. F. A. Burton in 1904. Below is the newly finished house of Fred S. Brown, of the pioneering Brown and Brothers Mercantile Company. The home was completed in 1907 at a cost of $12,000. This grand foursquare style stood on seven lots at the corner of Montview Boulevard and Claremont, and boasted 10 rooms, with two bathrooms and a billiard room in the basement. To the side stood the horse stable, with accommodations for the stable hands in the attic. (Above, *Denver Municipal Facts*, 1910; below, *Rocky Mountain News*, June 2, 1907, Denver Public Library, Western History Department.)

Several local newspapers competed for circulation in the early 1900s, including the *Denver Times*. In December 1901, the *Denver Times* ran a series of articles describing several types of houses that could be built for a moderate cost. "All articles and designs will be distinct in character," the *Denver Times* promised. This article featured a "Swiss Style Cottage" to cost $2,000, a foursquare with Swiss design elements This is a recent image of a similar "Swiss Style" house that was constructed in Park Hill. (Above, *Denver Municipal Facts*, 1911, Denver Public Library, Western History Department; below, Rebecca Dorward Collection.)

Near Twenty-third and Ash Streets, a more modest bungalow residence was constructed (shown above). Two innovations in 1912 dramatically changed the landscape of Park Hill: the introduction of the Ford Model T and the new electric car starter. With the new starter system, women could manage all aspects of driving and were not dependent on someone to crank the engine to start it. Dr. Margaret Long built the striking two-story house at 2070 Colorado Boulevard in 1909 (pictured below) and often drove by herself into the mountains for relief from her tuberculosis. She wrote about her explorations, and her books on historic western trails are filled with useful information. (Both, *Denver Municipal Facts*, 1911, Denver Public Library, Western History Department.)

This beautiful craftsman residence was built on Colorado Boulevard two blocks from Dr. Margaret Long's residence. The two-story porch extends to the side of the house, while French doors lead out to the second floor porch or balcony. The Fergusons, who completed the house in 1912, were probably standing near the steps in this photograph. Below is the same residence in 2003. Notice how little has changed. (Above, *Denver Municipal Facts,* 1911, Denver Public Library, Western History Department; below, Rebecca Dorward Collection.)

This beautiful 1910 home on Montview Boulevard was designed by architect Jules Jacques Benoit Benedict. It is known locally as the "Italian Spy House," because of its association with the Italian consul for the mountain states, Giovanni Formichella. In 1941, before Pearl Harbor, he was recalled to Rome after having violated zoning codes against having tenants on the property. There could be some truth to the "spy" label since a stash of radios and other electronic equipment was found in his basement. Recently, the owners have constructed a third story that cannot easily be seen from the street and an addition in the back. (Rebecca Dorward Collection.)

A great many buyers appeared to be average Denver residents, including middle-class workers and even wives. They often purchased the lots and hired a builder to construct the house, and the most popular style was the bungalow. By 1910, many bungalows were being built close to Montview Boulevard near the larger architect-designed homes. Bungalows occurred in many sizes and shapes. This Birch Street scene shows three similar houses with differing exteriors. A single electric car is parked along the street. (*Denver Municipal Facts*, 1910, Denver Public Library, Western History Department.)

The two interesting bungalows (page 26) still stand side by side. The residences today are the same as they were in 1910. They both contain craftsman elements in the facade treatments and the striking roof dormers. Bungalows were a new type of residence in the 1900s and quickly gained popularity because they could be constructed less expensively than other larger home styles, such as the Denver Square or the Victorian. (Both, Rebecca Dorward Collection.)

The price of a single lot increased from $150 in 1901 to about $300 in 1909, but since the width of a single lot was 25 feet, two lots were necessary to construct a house, and a location closer to Montview Boulevard also increased the price. During the beginning of the 20th century, as incomes began to rise, Denverites could find extra cash in savings accounts or cookie jars in order to purchase a two-lot parcel for $300 to $500. This photograph shows Montview Boulevard in 1910 looking west. The flat-topped building at the end of the street is the new City Park Museum, also seen below. (Both, *Denver Municipal Facts*, 1910, Denver Public Library, Western History Department.)

One of the most recognizable residences in Park Hill is this beautiful Tudor Revival built in 1908 at 2200 Ash Street and Twenty-second Avenue. Originally designed by architect William E. Fisher for Maurice and Emily Smith, it was extensively remodeled by Fisher in 1935 for the next owner, Alfred B. Trott, and his wife, Lena May. The half-timbering of the second story and roofing changes have made it very dramatic. Further alterations by architect Thomas Hart in 1990 led to the home's recognition in *Better Homes and Gardens*. The original Fisher-designed residence in 1908 called for a much different and smaller design. (Above, Rebecca Dorward Collection; below, *Denver Municipal Facts*, 1911, Denver Public Library, Western History Department.)

Many Park Hill houses included a brick horse barn or carriage house, and this structure sometimes reflected the same style as the house. They usually featured two wide wooden doors that could swing outward and contained an apartment above the barn. As automobiles began to replace horses and carriages, horse barns were typically converted into garages. Garage sizes and styles varied greatly. Nearly all were at the rear of the property, accessible through an alley. This is one of the more elaborate garages, having a full second floor with a balcony, decorative brickwork, and rooflines that date the structure to the early 1900s. Below, the brick Colonial Revival features two gargoyle-like sculptures ready to fly off the porch roof. Located close to Montview Boulevard, the house was featured in an early Park Hill home tour. (Both, Rebecca Dorward Collection.)

A striking French Eclectic residence, designed by local architect Maurice Biscoe, cost $8,000 in 1909. The original owners were a well-known doctor, Cuthbert Powell, and his wife, Mary. The socially prominent couple often entertained at their house. Live-in servants stayed on the third floor and moved around the house via a spiral stair, now removed. The Powells were enthusiastic supporters of the Denver Symphony Orchestra and donated a hand-carved wooden model of the 101-member orchestra in 1946. (Rebecca Dorward Collection.)

This photograph shows a completed street in Park Hill around 1910. Houses have been built on both sides of the street and landscaped with grass and small trees. The street has been cut lower than the lots to maintain the same street level as other streets and for better drainage. (*Denver Municipal Facts*, 1911, Denver Public Library, Western History Department.)

Another fine early residence, built at 4633 Montview Boulevard, is the Cones House, constructed in 1906. Designed by architects Richard Phillips and Edward Hess, the home boasts a distinctive round tower with a conical roof and cost $11,000 to complete. The owner, Homer C. Cones, made a fortune in the dry-goods business beginning in the 1890s. Later, in the 1970s, the building served as a monastery. In the 1990s, the current owners hired architect Douglas Walter to design a rear addition. This addition received an award in 1996 from the National Trust for Historic Preservation's Great American Home Awards for "sympathetic addition." (Above, *Denver Municipal Facts*, 1910, Denver Public Library, Western History Department; below, Rebecca Dorward Collection.)

This lovely image of a craftsman house on East Twenty-fifth Avenue was taken in 1911. The house combines round-arched windows with half-timbered dormers, a steeply pitched roof, and an inviting front porch. The corner location makes it eye-catching from two streets. Below is a charming example of a single-story bungalow with craftsman features in the porch and along the roof. The slanted brick piers and curved brickwork in the porch, the dramatic vergeboards extending from the porch roof, and the decorative wood treatments make this a wonderful example of craftsman styling. (*Denver Municipal Facts*, 1911, Denver Public Library, Western History Department.)

Some houses undergo remodeling over time. This Park Hill house was constructed as a Denver Square with a full-width front porch and a second-story balcony. At a later date, front porches grew out of style. This porch was removed, and the landscaping was altered. Now, without the porch, the detailed brickwork under the windows is more visible. A careful inspection of the facade shows the markings of the former porch attachments. Here and there in the neighborhood, a few other houses have had their porches removed. (Above, *Denver Municipal Facts,* 1911, Denver Public Library, Western History Department; below, Rebecca Dorward Collection.)

This large bungalow, at 2535 Dahlia Street, contains Tudor elements, such as the mock half-timbering on the second floor. Constructed for H. W. Huntington, the home sits on a raised lot with no trees, pointing to the newness of its construction. (*Denver Municipal Facts*, 1911, Denver Public Library, Western History Department.)

A small electric car is parked in City Park and overlooks the Park Hill development in the background. The automobile was first seen as a novelty for the rich, but as the years went by, cars became more important for everyone. The effect of the car on past culture can interestingly be compared to the effect of the Internet on today's culture. (*Denver Municipal Facts*, 1911, Denver Public Library, Western History Department.)

This striking architect-designed residence seems to be alone on its street. The interesting central roof dormer was probably designed for the live-in servants, who commonly stayed on the third floor and were provided a separate staircase down to the main levels. The flat roof, combined with the wide overhanging eaves, give this home an Italianate flare. Today the trees are larger and the landscaping more mature. (*Denver Municipal Facts*, 1911, Denver Public Library, Western History Department.)

Two

Hartman's Squares

Caspar Hartman was probably the first businessman to speculate in real estate east of Denver. In 1871, he platted Hartman's Addition, bounded by Colfax Avenue, Montview Boulevard, Colorado Boulevard, and Dahlia Street. Colfax Avenue was only a dirt road at the time, and the only transportation was horse-powered. No Denverites wanted to leave the comforts of home in town, such as running water, gas lighting, schools, churches, and even saloons. In fact, the Native American wars were still raging in other parts of the West. Only those who wished to operate a small farm or dairy were interested in life so far outside the safety of Denver. In spite of the obstacles, Hartman pushed forward with his speculative venture and laid out the streets, not in the typical rectangular blocks, but in square blocks that included one-fourth-acre lots. These lots were later divided into smaller parcels so that residences could have street access, and the centers of the blocks became community gardens, garage areas, or even a residence or two, accessed by alleyways. Hartman was a true optimist.

The Denver Orphan's Home originated in 1876 due to the high number of homeless children in Denver (as well as in other cities). It was sponsored by politically active women such as Margaret Evans, Elizabeth Byers and Elizabeth Hill Warren, and was originally located in this Victorian residence in Denver. (Denver Municipal Facts, 1911, Denver Public Library, Western History Department.)

By 1900, the home had become overcrowded, so a new facility was constructed at 1501 Albion Street, just north of Colfax Avenue in the Hartman's Addition. Along with sleeping rooms and classrooms, there were medical wards, and a nursery in the basement cared for infants. It is still in operation today, providing residential services for about 60 adolescents, with more extensive outpatient services reaching emotionally distressed children. It is now called the Denver Children's Home. (Denver Municipal Facts, 1911, Denver Public Library, Western History Department.)

This historical photograph shows young children outside the front of the Denver Children's Home all dressed in white and possibly participating in a dance or exercise. The recent photograph of the Denver Children's Home shows it to be remarkably like in was in 1902. No additions have been made to the structure. These days, the home serves about 60 residents and has an outpatient program to server another 150. (Above, *Denver Municipal Facts*, 1911, Denver Public Library, Western History Department; below, Rebecca Dorward Collection.)

This lovely Tudor Revival residence was actually built quite early in the development of Park Hill, around 1907. Located at 1980 Bellaire Street in Hartman's Addition, it was completed for $7,000, and contains a large yard typical of the Hartman's square blocks. According to the *Denver Municipal Facts* of 1910, the original owner could have been J. F. Montrose, who then sold it to Otis W. Lyman, who built his wealth as a hat maker. Early in the 1900s, Denver put on several farmers' markets and other celebrations in City Park. These fashionably dressed ladies pose for a picture in 1910 to celebrate Colorado Day, August 1, honoring statehood. (Above, *Denver Municipal Facts*, 1911; below, *Denver Municipal Facts*, 1910, Denver Public Library, Western History Department.)

This unprepossessing foursquare (above) stands on Montview Boulevard near Colorado Boulevard. It was designed by architect William E. Fisher in 1906 for wealthy attorney William Moore, his wife, Stella, and their daughter, Mildred. One day Stella ran off with the chauffeur, named John Smith, divorced her husband, and married Smith. The marriage eventually grew sour, due to Smith's gambling, drinking, and womanizing. In 1917, Stella went back to her previous husband and daughter. On January 13, 1917, the chauffeur forced his way into the house and began fighting with Stella. Some hours later, Stella shot John Smith twice with two different guns, and he died at the house. Stella was arrested and tried for murder in a sensational trial that rocked Denver. Her former husband came to her defense, hired psychiatric specialists, and helped her plead not guilty due to temporary insanity. The jury found her innocent, a victim of spousal abuse. The Moore house still stands today. (Above, Rebecca Dorward Collection; below, Tom Noel Collection.)

The Denver Square, or foursquare, became ubiquitous in Denver and could be built from floor plans in several popular catalogs such as the Sears or Montgomery Wards catalogs. A particular type of front porch was found in Park Hill Denver Squares, bungalows, and a few architect-designed homes in which the pillars supporting the porch roof extended through and above the roof. During the research for the Park Hill National Register Historic District, this type of porch support was unofficially named the "Park Hill Porch." The people of Denver and the area's suburbs enjoyed all the amenities of any American city at the beginning of the 20th century. The wind often kicked up dust from the dirt streets. This photograph below shows the street sprinkler wagon pulled by two horses. The wagon helped keep the dust down. (Above, Rebecca Dorward Collection; below, *Denver Municipal Facts*, 1910, Denver Public Library, Western History Department.)

carts are kept actively engaged
the day to prevent the accumula
refuse. These men are assign
squares and their foreman is he
ble for the cleanliness of that se

Nearly all of the streets in Park Hill were designed with alleyways for residents to reach for their horse-drawn carriages. Later, horse barns were simply converted into garages for cars. In the Hartman's Addition, the streets formed squares, not rectangles, and alleys were built around a central court, where an occasional small house was built. Such an alley house stands on the far left, behind the brick garage. (Rebecca Dorward Collection.)

Denver mayor Robert W. Speer was a forward-thinking politician. One of his favorite programs was known nationwide as the City Beautiful Movement. Speer promoted the construction of the parkways and parks in Park Hill and other areas of Denver. In addition, he annually held a tree giveaway, beginning in 1905. This photograph shows residents claiming their free trees to plant in their yards. Residents made a written application to the city and, if approved, would allow them three trees from three types: maple, elm, and North Carolina poplar. (*Denver Municipal Facts*, 1910, Denver Public Library, Western History Department.)

Through Mayor Robert Speer's influence, the City of Denver sponsored a Denver Play Carnival for several years in City Park, beginning in June 1911. In this photograph, the mayor is giving the opening speech for the outdoor event. Everyone was encouraged to attend. The Park Hill School and the Denver Orphan's Home both participated. Children competed in athletics, calisthenics displays, dance routines, and ball games. Each school erected a tent in the "tent city," where more than 600 children could congregate. The play carnivals took place for several years as the schools were ending for the summer. (*Denver Municipal Facts*, 1911, Denver Public Library, Western History Department.)

This image of the Denver Play Carnival shows groups of children and adults gathering at City Park. (*Denver Municipal Facts*, 1911, Denver Public Library, Western History Department.)

Robert W. Speer moved to Denver to the 1878 to find a cure for his tuberculosis. The Denver air proved restorative, and he got into politics, becoming mayor of the city in 1904. He made many improvements to parks and streets, and made enemies as well as friends. Today residents enjoy the results of his City Beautiful campaign, but at the time, many people were against the monetary expenditures. (*Denver Municipal Facts*, 1910, Denver Public Library, Western History Department.)

This lovely architect-designed residence is located on corner lots near Montview Boulevard. It reflects French Eclectic styling in the roof, with simple windows and two sculptures atop the roof supports. Above the porch roof is a balcony with a door from the second floor. The variety of housing styles and sizes in this neighborhood is truly remarkable. (Rebecca Dorward Collection.)

The Montclair Addition lies just to the east and south of Park Hill. It was platted by Baron Manfred von Richtofen, who built a stone castle for his residence and brought transportation out to his development. This photograph shows a city playground established in Montclair with city funding. It was considered one of the best playgrounds in Denver. (*City of Denver*, 1914, Denver Public Library, Western History Department.)

Three

EXCLUSIVE DOWNINGTON

Pioneer attorney Jacob M. Downing moved to Denver in 1859, when the town consisted of a few wooden shacks at the confluence of the South Platte River and Cherry Creek. He had a successful law career, and in 1886, he bought and platted Downington, near Hartman's Addition. The Colfax Avenue Railway operated at that time, and Downing worked to extend it farther into his development. Later he partnered with another up-and-coming lawyer named Warwick M. Downing, who was part of Denver mayor Robert W. Speer's City Beautiful movement. The two attorneys (unrelated), pushed for trees, parks, and parkways in Downington, and by the early 1900s, their development was a true showcase. The local newspaper, the *Rocky Mountain News*, called it "swell" in its July 19, 1907, edition. Many stylish and grand homes were built along the Seventeenth Avenue Parkway. The Downington Addition was platted without alleys, with garage access through driveways from the street. Many boulevards and parkways were added during Denver's City Beautiful days in the early 1900s. Speculators agreed to restrictive covenants in Downington, such as no apartments, stores, or even hospitals. Only expensive homes could be constructed, and residents should be "white householders only." (*Denver Municipal Facts, 1909*, Denver Public Library, Western History Department, Noel and Hansen, 2002.)

This photograph, taken at Seventeenth Avenue and Hudson Street, shows the newly paved Seventeenth Avenue Parkway, with trees planted between the curbs and sidewalks. In the background stands the 1907 Hayden house and the 1909 Tudor Revival–style Cook house. Below is a close-up of the Hayden house, built by G. W. Huntington for Lewis Hayden and his family. Hayden was a successful mining engineer in the Cripple Creek mining district. The second floor of this house contained four bedchambers, and the third floor accommodated the servants for the family, while the first floor contained an aviary. Outside stood a tennis court and a six-car garage, now demolished. (Both, *Denver Municipal Facts,* 1910, Denver Public Library, Western History Department.)

The City of Denver oiled the streets in Park Hill and created concrete curbs and sidewalks around 1909. Some of the original sidewalk stamps from local concrete companies can still be seen on the sidewalks of Montview Boulevard and Ash Street. In this photograph, street workers grade a street in Downington. (Denver Public Library, Western History Department.)

In the vicinity of Bellaire Street and Sixteenth Avenue, local builders constructed this row of bungalows in 1910. The lots are smaller than those on or near Montview Boulevard. Extremely substantial and comfortable inside and out, these homes have stood the test of time. (*Denver Municipal Facts*, 1910, Denver Public Library, Western History Department.)

Built in the early 1890s, this simple Queen Anne–style Victorian residence is one of the oldest houses remaining in the Downington Addition. The Obrecht family emigrated from Switzerland and settled on a few acres in Downington. From this location, the family operated the Park Hill Dairy. In the early 1900s, they opened a store in Denver to sell the dairy products and produce. The front-gabled house is similar to the Victorian house on Thirty-fifth Avenue and Albion Street. Several additions to the structure have not obscured the Victorian original on the Seventeenth Avenue Parkway. (*Denver Municipal Facts*, 1911, Denver Public Library, Western History Department.)

The City of Denver apparently operated its own dairy, named the City Park Dairy Farm. In the late 1800s and early 1900s, tainted milk became a source of major health problems. Cities around the country promoted cleaner practices at dairies and for the milk delivery businesses. (*Denver Municipal Facts,* 1911, Denver Public Library, Western History Department.)

The most impressive Windsor Farm Dairy was downtown located just east and south of Park Hill. It had operated in the 1880s to sell dairy goods to the downtown Windsor Hotel. The large-scale operation required many employees. In Denver, deliverymen and their wagons gather outside the company warehouse. (*Denver Municipal Facts*, 1911, Denver Public Library, Western History Department.)

For an area the size of Denver and its suburbs, many dairies were required. The Montclair Dairy was one of the closest to Park Hill and was one of the best dairies for sanitary practices. Originated by Baron Manfred von Richtofen, the large barn is still standing today as the Montclair Community Center. (*Denver Municipal Facts*, 1911, Denver Public Library, Western History Department.)

Two newspapers, the *Rocky Mountain News* and the *Denver Times*, collaborated in a 1907 contest in which the grand prize was the construction of a $5,000 house. The newspapers were promoting the fashionable Denver Square style, which was to be built on two lots in Downington. (Rebecca Dorward Collection.)

The early residents of Colorado were patriotic and enthusiastic about their state. Every August 1, celebrations took place marking Colorado Day, honoring the day that Colorado obtained statehood in 1876. At City Park, original pioneer William H. Green raised the state flag for the Colorado Day celebrations. This day is still celebrated with speeches and local events. (*Denver Municipal Facts*, 1911, Denver Public Library, Western History Department.)

Denver was fortunate to employ important landscape architect Saco R. DeBoer to help create the area's parks and parkways, such as Montview Boulevard, Seventeenth Avenue Parkway, and Forest Street Parkway, all in Park Hill. DeBoer also provided the landscape designs for several prominent residences in Park Hill, such as the Hall house on Montview Boulevard. (*Denver Municipal Facts*, 1911, Denver Public Library, Western History Department.)

In 1912, architects Ernest and Lester Varian completed this Mediterranean Revival–style residence for owner Frederick G. Walsen on the Seventeenth Avenue Parkway. His father, Gen. Frederick Walsen, had been an early explorer who had founded the town of Walsenburg. The Walsens raised three children while Frederick G. Walsen headed the American Bank and Trust Company. (*Denver Municipal Facts*, 1912, Denver Public Library, Western History Department.)

Denver was a city filled with hospitality, and the residents loved nothing better than a good parade down Sixteenth or Seventeenth Streets. A recurring event was the Festival of Mountain and Plain, which lasted several days and promoted many local companies. This photograph shows a Studebaker Company float in the Festival of Mountain and Plain of 1912. One year later, the Knights Templar held their Grand Conclave in Denver and had their own parade down Sixteenth Street. (Both, *Denver Municipal Facts*, 1912, 1913, Denver Public Library, Western History Department.)

Another parade in downtown Denver brought out everyone to celebrate the end of World War I after the Colorado soldiers had returned home. The war had affected a great many Colorado families and to provide medical care for injured soldiers, the Fitzimons Army Hospital had been constructed east of Park Hill. (*Denver Municipal Facts*, 1918, Denver Public Library, Western History Department.)

This lovely home, designed by Burnham and Merril Hoyt, was constructed on Forest Street Parkway on the western edge of Downington in 1928. Located north of Colfax Avenue, Forest Street Parkway was a two-block section between Seventeenth Avenue and Montview Boulevard that had received extra landscaping and a park-like median. (Denver Public Library, Western History Department.)

Four

More's Park Heights and Other Additions

Zophar W. More platted More's Park Heights in 1888 adjacent to Hartman's Addition, and that same year, he and several associates incorporated the Park Railway Line to bring transportation to the area along the northern boundary at Twenty-third Avenue. In 1893, an economic depression caused the residential boom to end and the railway to stop running. Several years later, the Denver Tramway Company took over this railway in its attempt to unify the transportation system. The economy gradually improved after 1900. Other developments occurred with Cook's Addition, Strayers Park Heights, Chamberlin and Winne's, and Colfax Heights, until the entire area was platted. Either by custom or by restrictive covenants, only white families were allowed to live in the newly established neighborhoods. In reality, however, several black families owned homes in Park Hill in the 1890s and 1900s near the end of the transportation line at Twenty-third Avenue and Holly Street, and some had a few extra acres for raising farm animals and vegetables. Possibly the first black couple was Hamilton and Mary Brown, who bought land at 2420 Clermont Street in 1892 and later built a small house there. Another homeowner, Zenon Brickler, was a well-established black barber in Denver who owned his business and built his house on Twenty-ninth and Dahlia Streets in 1895. He and his wife, May, raised 11 children there. It has since been demolished.

The Hall house, located on Montview Boulevard and Fairfax Street, remains one of Park Hill's most splendid residences. Designed by architect William A. Cowe in 1906 for John A. Beeler and his family, it contains leaded-glass windows, crystal light fixtures, and an elaborate intercom system. Beeler worked as vice president and general manager of the Denver Tramway Company, the one entity that suburban areas needed to provide transportation into Denver. He moved away in 1916, and the property was sold to an oilman, Joseph J. Hall. His daughter Josephine is shown on this book's cover. Hall made improvements to the home, such as the extensive landscaping by Saco R. DeBoer. (*Denver Municipal Facts,* 1911, Denver Public Library, Western History Department.)

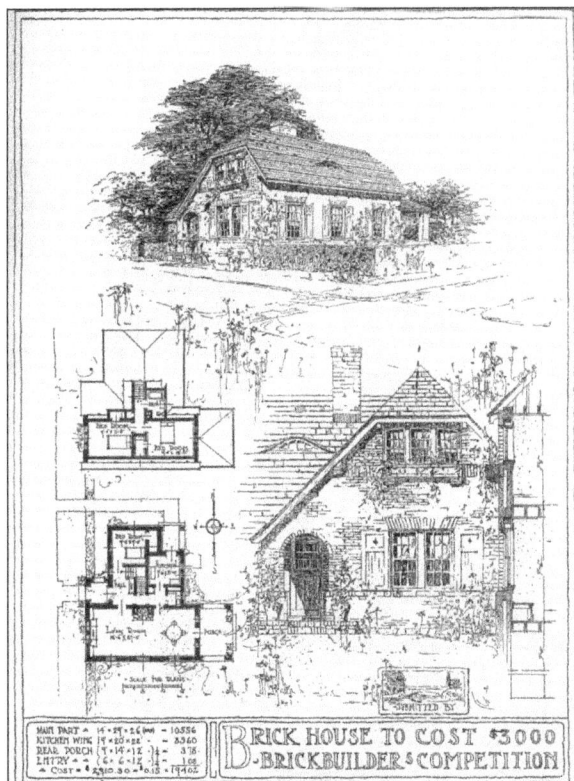

In 1911, two prominent architectural firms, Fisher and Fisher, and Maurice Biscoe, designed four small houses, each in the 2500 block of Dexter Street. Below is a photograph of one possible contest house. These small houses were all built on speculation with asking prices around $3,000 in 1911–1912, and could have represented entries into the national contest for small-house designs held by the Brick Institute in 1912. (Both, Rebecca Dorward Collection.)

At the northern limits of Park Hill, development proved slower, and parts of it appeared to be open prairie. This is an early photograph of a child in a stroller at a house on Thirty-fifth Avenue and Albion Street around 1910. This area was served by a horse-drawn trolley into downtown Denver. (National Register of Historic Places, Rebecca Dorward Collection.)

The Strayer Real Estate and Investment Company worked to sell the lots in Strayer's Park Heights. One of the newspaper advertisements of the day stated, "None can offer such inducements to investors as we are now doing in these Most Beautiful Additions. Every lot is perfect; so full of charm and beauty, owing to the elevation (200 feet above the center of city) and location in full view of City Park, the city and entire range of the Rockies . . . THE PARK RAILWAY-RAPID TRANSIT LINE, best built and most elegantly equipped line of our metropolis, passes directly through these suburbs." (Denver Municipal Facts, 1911, Denver Public Library, Western History Department.)

Advertising in the 1890s and early 1900s was longwinded at best. Another Strayer's advertisement said, "BEAR IN MIND THAT REAL ESTATE IS THE BASIS OF ALL WEALTH. As we absolutely refuse to place on our books any property that has not merit to commend it to an investor, either as to location or price, we feel assured all parties Investing through us will be greatly benefitted. . . . We take great pleasure in showing our property, having both a double and single team always at our command, and it is neither trouble nor cost. 'THE EARLY BIRD CATCHES THE WORM.'" This engine-powered touring vehicle was one of the "Seeing Denver" vehicles that drove around the town, introducing people to other parts of Denver. (*Denver Municipal Facts*, 1911.)

Denver's most popular department store was arguably the Daniels and Fisher Department Store, in which everything from light fixtures to clothes could be purchased and delivered in a timely fashion right to a person's front door. The D&F Tower proved to be a Denver landmark from the time of its construction and remains so today. (Both, *Denver Municipal Facts,* 1911, Denver Public Library, Western History Department.)

In 1908, a large craftsman-style bungalow was completed at Twenty-third Avenue and Eudora Street for businessman Charles O. Johnson. The two dormers seem to extend down into the front porch roof and are quite eye-catching. In 1938, William E. and Louise Turnbull purchased the house, and their family still lives there. Turnbull and his wife owned and operated Rainbow Pictures, making and animating films. (*Denver Municipal Facts*, 1910, Denver Public Library, Western History Department.)

This lovely craftsman-style house was built at 4705 East Twenty-fifth Avenue in 1910. One of the first owners was M. Kingsbury. The corner lot positioning made the backyard smaller than others in the area, and the garage was reached from the far side of the house. (*Denver Municipal Facts*, 1910, Denver Public Library, Western History Department.)

A row of single-story bungalows stands as efficiently today as they did 90 years ago. This longevity attests to the functionality and livability of this housing style, which can be found in every American city. (Rebecca Dorward Collection.)

Occasionally a smaller house was constructed at the rear of its lot, closer to the alley than the street. This was more likely to occur in Hartman's Addition, but it also could be found in other parts of Park Hill. Some detached garages were eventually made into second houses or apartments, as well. (Rebecca Dorward Collection.)

Five

TRANSPORTATION

TO AND FROM

To develop a plat of barren land miles from the city of Denver in the 1880s and 1890s required speculators to plan ahead and have patience. The Park Hill lands were north of the only through road, Colfax Avenue. Wealthy families owned horses and buggies, but that method of transportation was slow and undesirable to use on a daily basis. If families were going to move to Park Hill, a convenient, inexpensive form of public transportation was needed to take residents to and from downtown Denver. Although public transportation first began in Denver in 1871, the route was limited to a short, single horsecar line in downtown Denver. Additional routes and horse-less forms of electric and cable cars soon expanded service within Denver. Jacob Downing realized that his addition would be more desirable if it was accessible to the downtown business streets, so he invested in the newly established Colfax Avenue Railway Car Company. In 1887, standard-gauge streetcar tracks were laid from York Street east to Quebec Street in Montclair. However, service west from York Street did not connect to service into Denver. After many arguments and meetings, the Denver City Railway Company agreed to lay track between its terminal in Denver and York Street. Service began late in December 1887 using horsecars along Colfax Avenue out to Quebec Street.

In suburbs such as Park Hill and Montclair, transportation routes had to be cut out of the prairie, then track laid for the cars. Looking west across both Montclair and Park Hill, two cross streets are marked by telephone poles and fence posts. (*Denver Municipal Facts*, 1910, Denver Public Library, Western History Department.)

In 1888, the Denver Tramway Company brought cable cars into Denver along Broadway and Colfax Avenues. For a time, both horsecars and cable cars ran out to York Street, but only the horsecars continued to Quebec Street. Other methods of transportation were often preferred by those who could afford their own horse and buggy or automobile. (*Denver Municipal Facts*, 1910, Denver Public Library, Western History Department.)

Businessman Zophar More began public transportation that weaved through the various Park Hill additions until the end at East Thirty-second Avenue in More's Park Heights. The one-way fare was 5¢. This company used steam power, called "steam-dummy" locomotives, which were a smaller version of a passenger car and were touted to be quiet. A major danger in towns at that time was of horses being spooked by unusual sights and sounds. Horses could become unmanageable, causing accidents and even deaths. The "steam-dummy" looked like a horsecar and was quiet, so horses would not be upset. This image shows the Cook line near Colorado Boulevard with a missing horse. (*Denver Municipal Facts*, 1910, Denver Public Library, Western History Department.)

The Capitol Hill Land Company laid tracks along Thirty-fourth Avenue east to Colorado Boulevard and into Park Hill in 1892. Two horses pulled the car and trailer up the hill on Thirty-fourth Avenue to the top of the hill at Cook Street. There the trailer was uncoupled and parked, and the horses continued pulling the passenger car eastward. On the return trip, the horses pulled the car to Cook Street, where the trailer was reattached to the car, the horses climbed into the trailer, and the cars quickly ran downhill to the west end of the line at Gaylord Street. Along the Twenty-third Avenue line through Park Hill, horses probably endured similar conditions to horses on the Cherrelyn line. This famous horsecar route operated in Englewood, where the horses rode downhill on the return routes. (Both, *Denver Municipal Facts*, 1909, Denver Public Library, Western History Department.)

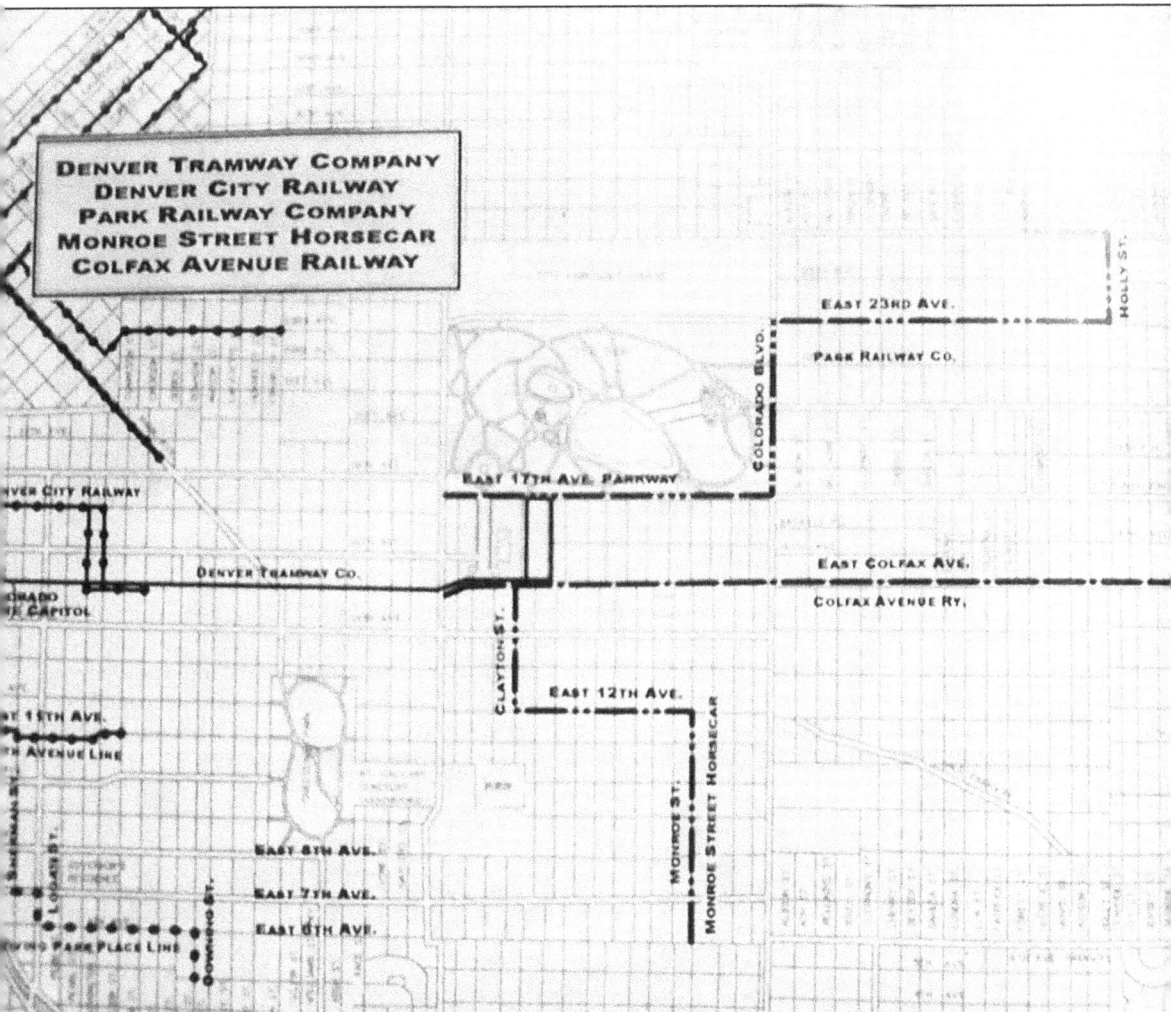

The competitive environment of Denver gave rise to several transportation companies and various forms of transportation, such as horsecars, electric cars, cable cars, and trolleys. Eventually, the Denver Tramway Company consolidated most of the lines and streamlined the routes for people. This map shows the routes used by the Denver Tramway Company around 1910. (*Denver Municipal Facts*, 1910, Denver Public Library, Western History Department.)

The Denver Tramway Company was operating along Colfax Avenue in 1903 using cable cars, while the horsecar line stood on the right side of the cable car tracks. Some streets became a jumble of various cable car lines and overhead electric lines. As the companies consolidated into the Denver Tramway Company and technologies were standardized into cable cars, the situation became less haphazard, as in the photograph of the Park Hill cable car. (Colorado Railroad Museum.)

Around 1912, the City of Denver invested in the most modern types of transportation to update services to the neighborhoods. This group of policemen was known as the Motorcycle Emergency Squad. In this photograph, the squad displays the new motorcycles for the camera. (*City of Denver*, 1913, Denver Public Library, Western History Department.)

DENVER'S NEW AUTO PATROL WAGON.

Park Hill was annexed into the City of Denver in 1903, and from that time forward, the city has provided services such as fire and police. In the early 1900s, police vehicles, such as the one shown above, patrolled the streets and parkways of Park Hill. This vehicle came equipped with a spotlight and a bell to alert traffic and an enclosed cabin place for alleged offenders to safely ride to the police station. (*Denver Municipal Facts*, 1910, Denver Public Library, Western History Department.)

The Denver Fire Department served Park Hill for fires and other emergencies. This image shows an original hand pump fire engine first used by the City of Denver, while below is the 1911 transportation style of Denver's fire officers. Notice the bell on top of the engine hood. (*Denver Municipal Facts*, 1911, Denver Public Library, Western History Department.)

Fire station No. 18, completed in 1912, served the Park Hill area from Colorado Boulevard at a corner of City Park. Designed by architect Edwin H. Moorman, Mayor Robert W. Speer promoted the unique bungalow styling and its controversial location on City Park land. Bungalows were so popular in Park Hill that this new station could fit right in. Notice the two classic bungalow elements of the eyebrow dormers and the entrance pergola. Below is Denver's fire station No. 1, shown in 1911 and located in downtown Denver. Beautification projects such as this one occurred on many city properties. The Beaux-Arts styling of the facade is enhanced by the flower boxes along the second-floor windows. (Above, *Denver Municipal Facts*, 1911; below, *Denver Municipal Facts*, 1912, Denver Public Library, Western History Department.)

The Tramway Company offered transportation services to Denverites for decades. These photographs show cable cars that ran along the Twenty-third Avenue route in Park Hill. The image above shows car No. 827, and an advertisement on the front states," Give a Meal, Save a Life," while the image below shows a cable car during World War II, with a sign on the side stating, "Lets Get It Over" and "Buy More War Bonds." (Both, Colorado Railroad Museum.)

In the 1920s, Americans felt great enthusiasm for the new adventure called flying. Pilots who owned airplanes often set up in a vacant field and took people up for rides for a price. In 1924, Lowry Field began operations north of Park Hill on Thirty-eighth and Dahlia Streets. (Wings over the Rockies Air and Space Museum.)

This image shows a rare aerial view of old Lowry Field around 1930. The letters on top of the hangar give the name. Located near the two hangars are several tents for use by the National Guard squadron stationed there. (Wings over the Rockies Air and Space Museum.)

Just three years later, Charles A. Lindbergh flew into Lowry Field in his *Spirit of St. Louis*, and the airplane was paraded down Colorado Boulevard to promote flying. Then, one year later, Amelia Earhart also flew into Lowry Field. The field was moved eastward in 1938, but that was not the end of Park Hill's association with flying. (*Denver Municipal Facts*, Denver Public Library, Western History Department.)

This aerial view shows a biplane flying over the Park Hill and Montclair neighborhoods with a stuntman dangling from a lower wing. On the far left is a partial view of one of the Colorado Women's College buildings. (Wings over the Rockies Air and Space Museum.)

In 1929, the Denver Municipal Airport began operations on a large site just east of Park Hill. For decades, air traffic passed over the Park Hill neighborhood. This photograph shows how close the old Lowry Field was to the new municipal airport. (Wings over the Rockies Air and Space Museum.)

Our squadron on Lowry Field, Denver, Colo.

Another rare photograph shows a ground view of Lowry Field with a row of Douglas O-2 National Guard biplanes parked on the grass. The stripes on the rudders indicate they were built before 1926. A few cars are parked next to the hangars. (Wings over the Rockies Air and Space Museum.)

As commercial aviation came into its own, the Denver Municipal Airport expanded and changed its name to Stapleton Airfield in 1941 in honor of Denver mayor Benjamin F. Stapleton. Eventually the airport added more runways, hangars, and terminals, and became Stapleton International Airport. This image shows both the original control tower (on the left), and the newer, taller control tower, with commercial jets from Continental Airlines and United Airlines. Denver is still the headquarters of United Airlines. (Wings over the Rockies Air and Space Museum, 1970s.)

A National Guard squadron of biplanes flies overhead at the new Denver Municipal airport around 1929, while a monoplane is shown possibly taxiing into the large hangar. Notice the period cars parked near the hangar. This photograph is probably from the opening ceremonies for the new airport. (*Denver Municipal Facts*, 1929, Denver Public Library, Western History Department.)

Six

AROUND THE
NEIGHBORHOOD

Today's Park Hill is a 20th-century neighborhood. Although a few self-sufficient families had moved in before 1900, the vast majority of residences and institutions were the products of the 20th century. The first school, Park Hill School, was built in 1901 and has been expanded more than once to accommodate increased enrollments. Additional schools were built as needed. Several early religious congregations met in public halls or even tents before the church buildings were constructed. By the time of automobile popularity, after 1912, church attendance was growing rapidly. In conjunction with the church groups, the Park Hill Improvement Association originated about 1906 to foster community awareness and to maintain certain restrictions or covenants written into the original plats. Eventually, the restrictions were abandoned. The neighborhood developed a close connection with flying and airports, and saw its prestige grow as one of the most desirable suburbs in Denver.

At the beginning of the 20th century, cities became aware of the need to provide certain services to residential and business areas. Sanitation in all its forms became a major issue, and Denver dealt with the issues by having a sanitation department and inspectors to inspect complaints. The sanitary inspector was provided a modern vehicle and even a driver. (*Denver Municipal Facts*, 1912, Denver Public Library, Western History Department.)

A typical bungalow in Park Hill, constructed in 1912, shows the centered front door, balanced by the front windows, and the substantial porch has double porch supports, or piers, and a large bedroom dormer upstairs. (*Denver Municipal Facts*, 1912, Denver Public Library, Western History Department.)

The State of Colorado passed an architect licensing law in 1909. Before that, building contractors were able to design and construct any type of structure. After 1909, several builders passed the license requirements and became practicing architects, while others continued to construct residences without the use of an architect design. William E. Fisher designed this lovely Georgian Revival–style residence on Montview Boulevard. (Rebecca Dorward Collection.)

Many of Denver's most prominent architects contributed to the neighborhood's growth, among them William E. and Arthur A. Fisher, Burnham F. and Merril H. Hoyt, Jules Jacque B. Benedict, Maurice B. Biscoe, Frank Edbrooke, Montana S. Fallis, Robert S. Roeschlaub, and Glen H. and Daniel R. Huntington. This lovely craftsman home was completed in 1910 on Twenty-second Avenue and Hudson Street. (*Denver Municipal Facts*, 1910, Denver Public Library, Western History Department.)

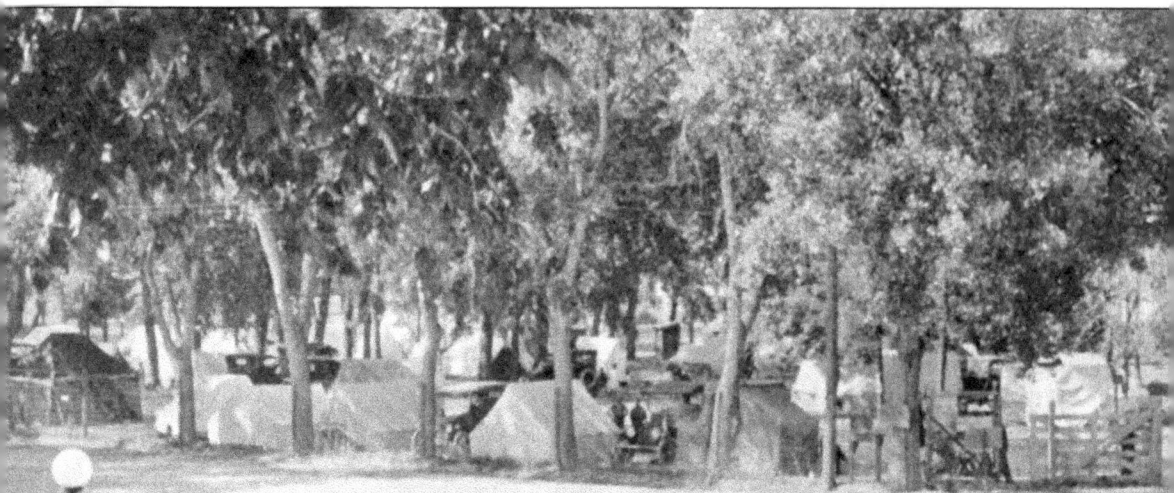

The Great Spring Drive

Motordom's Annual Migration Soon to Start—
Denver's Tent City the Half-way House

The automobile became popular within a few years of the introduction of the Ford Model T. This view shows a free car camp set up in City Park in 1918. Tourists were able to pitch a tent and stay overnight. (Denver Public Library, Western History Department.)

Denver's City Park, adjacent to Park Hill on the west side of Colorado Boulevard, provided recreational opportunities for residents all year long. This image was taken in 1909 and shows local children ice-skating on the frozen City Park Lake, which is covered in a dusting of snow. The smaller girl in the foreground and the boy to the right behind her are wearing double-bladed skates, a type of training skate. (*Denver Municipal Facts*, 1909, Denver Public Library, Western History Department.)

The blizzard of December 1913 dropped 3 to 4 feet of snow along the Front Range and brought Denver and the surrounding area to a standstill. It lasted from Monday, December 1 until Saturday, December 6, and strong winds blew the snows into drifts as high as 20 feet. Thousands of people were stranded inside public buildings and on streetcars. Volunteers brought supplies to hospitals and orphanages. The Denver Tramway Company sent out 4,000 employees to dig the snow out of the streets, put it into horse-drawn wagons, and haul it to the Civic Center Park. At least 14 buildings were crushed under the weight of the snow, and records indicate at least 34 people died. Some of the snow dumped in Civic Center Park did not melt until spring. When the snow melted, major flooding occurred in streets and inside houses. The image to the left shows a resident standing on top of the snow. The photograph below shows tramway employees working on Tremont Street. (Above, Rebecca Dorward Collection; below, *City of Denver*, 1913, Denver Public Library, Western History Department.)

Several orphanages existed in the Denver area around the beginning of the 20th century. This home for homeless boys was launched in 1911 as the Clayton College for Boys. A charitable gift from pioneer George W. Clayton, the home was established after Clayton's death, with oversight by the City of Denver. The home north of City Gark opened in 1912 "to be devoted solely and exclusively to the founding, establishing, and forever maintaining a permanent College . . . for the better education, and more comfortable maintenance" of young white boys whose fathers had died and whose mothers were unable to care for them. Operating from 1911 through 1957, approximately 600 individual boys were sent there, aged 6 to 14. This image shows the administration building just after its completion in 1912. Below is a view of the school layout. (Above, Rebecca Dorward Collection; below, *Denver Municipal Facts*, 1911, Denver Public Library, Western History Department.)

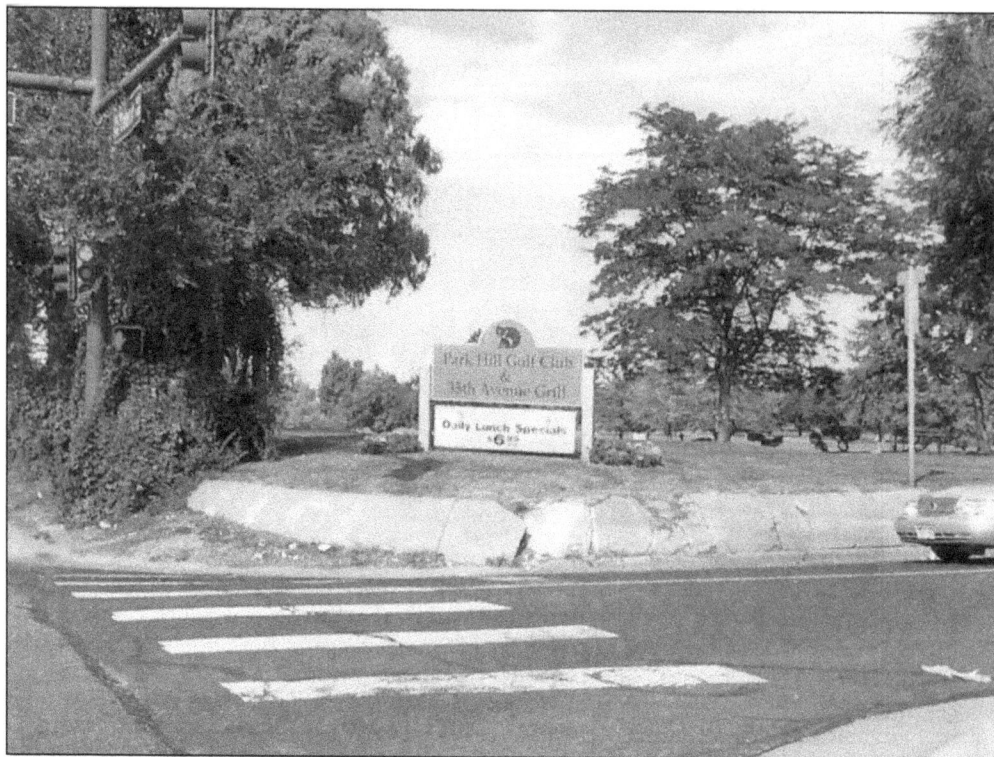

The Clayton College Dairy Farm was located across Colorado Boulevard from the campus. Today the city-owned Park Hill Golf Course is located where the dairy once stood. Built in 1932, it had a Tudor-style clubhouse that was later replaced by a modern facility. (Rebecca Dorward Collection.)

Even in 1912, schoolchildren were eager to celebrate birthdays of past presidents. This image speaks of early patriotism, as the children dress in self-made hats and parade around the classroom. (*Denver Municipal Facts*, 1912, Denver Public Library, Western History Department.)

In 1921, a group of local architects created the Mountain Division, Inc., of the Architects' Small House Bureau in Denver. Architect William E. Fisher served as the first president. Several architects joined this organization to provide superior house plans to middle-class families at a nominal cost. These small houses were basically no frills, usually built without wide overhanging eaves or ornamentation, as in the model dubbed "the H&H Baby Grand," advertised by the Hallack and Howard Lumber Company. At least one baby grand house was completed in Park Hill. The advertisement boasted a stucco exterior and tile roof, and this house qualifies. Another cost-cutting feature included the short front porch piers. (Above, Denver Public Library, Western History Department; below, Rebecca Dorward Collection.)

One of Denver's oldest high schools is still going strong—East High School near Colfax Avenue. This image, taken in 1909, shows the Romanesque styling of old East High. Though it was demolished in 1925, the newer East High, built in the same year, is considered extremely significant and was designated a Historic Denver Landmark in 1991. East High has always served the Park Hill neighborhood and surrounding areas. Many famous people have attended this school, including actors Douglas Fairbank, Sr., Hattie McDaniel, Don Cheadle, and Antoinette Perry (namesake of the Tony Awards), author Sidney Sheldon, and astronaut Jack Swigert. (Above, *Denver Municipal Facts*, 1909, Denver Public Library, Western History Department; below, East High School, Denver Public School District.)

By 1914, the Natural History Museum and grounds began to take shape, as this image shows. Cars are parked along the front steps as visitors come and go. Today this building still remains, although it has been extensively remodeled. (*City of Denver*, 1914, Denver Public Library, Western History Department.)

In 1900, local residents organized a Presbyterian congregation and purchased land at the corner of Dahlia Street and the south side of Montview Boulevard. This had been the location of the DuPont gunpowder storage plant, which had been destroyed in 1884. The local church members cleared the site and, in 1902, erected a canvas tent with a wood floor as the first church. The following year, the congregation purchased the former 1893 Park School for $500 and relocated the frame building to the church site to serve as the sanctuary. In 1910, with an expanding membership, the congregation built a new chapel on the site using stones from the recently demolished Central Presbyterian Church, which had stood downtown at Eighteenth and Champa Streets. In 1918, local architects Harry James Manning and Francis W. Frewan designed and built a new Gothic and Romanesque Revival–style church, which incorporated a three-story square tower with a castellated parapet. (*Guidon*, 1911, Denver Public Library, Western History Department.)

Fortunately for the historic record, the newly established Montview Boulevard Presbyterian Church began publishing a monthly bulletin in 1908 filled with local news about residents of Park Hill. On a pleasant Sunday in October 1911, the Presbyterian membership held a Rally Day. The brainchild of a church member, 15 cars and drivers motored around the Park Hill streets bringing churchgoers to Montview Boulevard Presbyterian Church for the Sunday service. Return rides were guaranteed, and everyone had an enjoyable time. In 1911, with the automobile still a novelty, many people were excited to ride in a car. The event proved so popular that a second Rally Day was held the following October. (*Guidon*, 1911, 1912, Denver Public Library, Western History Department.)

Children from the Presbyterian Sunday school pose with their instruments for a cover of the *Guidon* in 1912. The Montview congregation took a strong role in the education of children and adolescents. Young people were encouraged to attend Sunday school and participate in the church activities. (*Guidon*, 1912, Denver Public Library, Western History Department.)

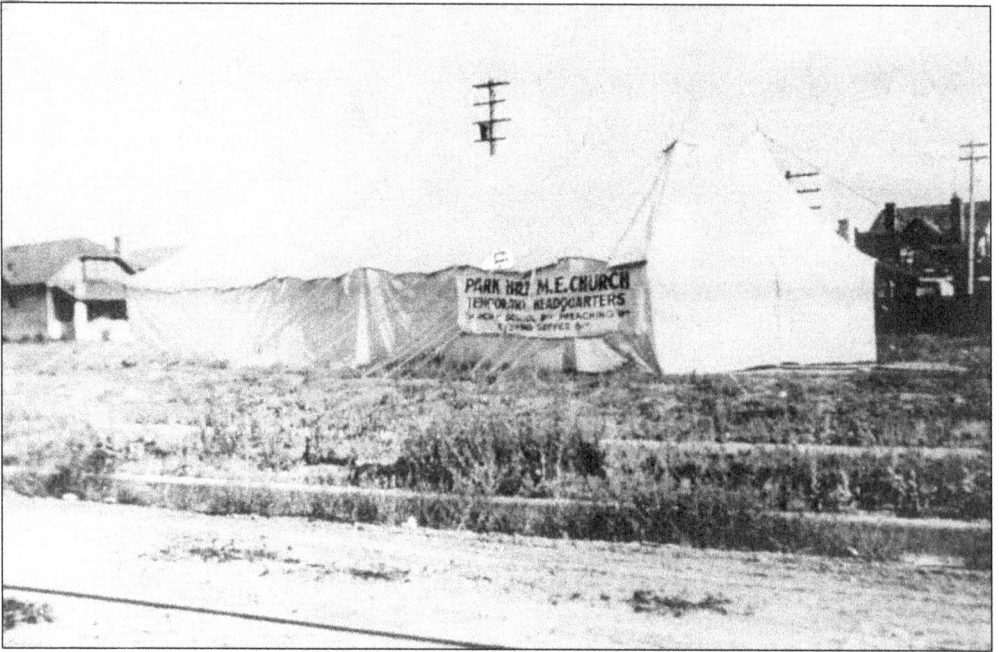

In 1910, a Methodist congregation, which had been meeting in Denver, purchased lots on vacant land along the north side of Twenty-third Avenue at Dexter Street, and a tent was erected for worship services. The membership began to grow quickly, and a permanent building was soon needed. (Tom Noel Collection.)

The following year, in 1911, an impressive brick church, designed by Charles M. Gates, was constructed at the site. The congregation had challenged itself to finish the building in 100 days, and that task was accomplished. (*Denver Municipal Facts*, 1911, Denver Public Library, Western History Department.)

The Romanesque Revival–style Methodist church boasted a three-story bell tower and castellated parapets, along with a full basement that contained a gymnasium. This sanctuary served the congregation for about 10 years. (*Denver Municipal Facts*, 1911, Denver Public Library, Western History Department.)

A problem arose when developer Charles R. Maddox of the Crescent Realty Company purchased adjacent lots and planned to erect several single-story shops along Twenty-third Avenue across from the Methodist church. The general opinion of the residents was that commercial operations within Park Hill would lead to a depreciation of property values, a terrible situation for the residents. In spite of neighborhood opposition, developer Charles Maddox constructed his commercial shopping area in 1913 along the busy streetcar route. Produce and meat shops, a creamery, and a tailor shop occupied the storefronts. (Rebecca Dorward Collection.)

By 1921, the expanded church membership decided to relocate to its current site at 5209 Montview Boulevard, while retaining the existing land and building. In a splendid example of adaptive reuse, the old church structure was renovated and enlarged for use as apartments and shops. The conversion actually kept the bell tower, the entrance, and certain windows, while adding new wings for the storefronts along Twenty-third Avenue. The Park Hill Drug Store first occupied the corner location, and a Piggly Wiggly grocery store moved in next door. The grocery offered something new for shoppers in Denver—self-service shopping. Today the Cherry Tomato restaurant occupies the drugstore site and Spinelli's Market the Piggly Wiggly storefront. (Rebecca Dorward Collection.)

With the decision to move the church away from the shops along Twenty-third Avenue, the congregation acquired land along Montview Boulevard and, in 1924, completed the present Park Hill United Methodist Church. Architect William N. Bowman designed the original Mission Revival–style structure and Philips-Carter Reister the alterations in 1968. It has a four-story domed bell tower and a 500-seat sanctuary with stained-glass windows. In 1968, the head pastor was J. Carlton Babbs, who took a lead role in promoting integration in the Park Hill neighborhood. A community award is now named in his honor. (Both, Rebecca Dorward Collection.)

In 1913, a neoclassical church was completed for the Catholic families of Park Hill. It was dedicated as Blessed Sacrament Catholic Church, located on Montview Boulevard. In 1915, Blessed Sacrament launched its locally famous Easter Monday Ball at the Brown Palace Hotel, a fund-raiser that helped pay for a school staffed by the Sisters of Loretto and a three-story brick rectory in 1923. (*Denver Municipal Facts,* 1913, Denver Public Library, Western History Department.)

As Park Hill emerged as one of Denver's most prestigious subdivisions in the 1920s, Blessed Sacrament Catholic Church hired Denver architect Harry James Manning to design an elaborate $250,000 neo-Gothic church. However, the crash of 1929 and ensuing economic depression put plans on hold. Manning died in 1933, and his associate, William E. Andress, was asked to scale down the project. Today Blessed Sacrament remains an interesting example of the English Gothic style. Although it has been remodeled several times, surviving original elements include the Gothic grand entry and exquisite stained-glass windows from a German artist in Munich. (Rebecca Dorward Collection.)

St. Thomas Episcopal Church was completed in 1908 as a simple brick church, but in 1930, architect Harry James Manning remodeled the church in the Spanish Colonial Revival style. It has one of the most beautiful and welcoming entryways in Denver. Off the beaten path between Montview Boulevard and Twenty-third Avenue, its location belies its social significance as one of Denver's first racially integrated congregations and as one of the first churches to allow women and girls opportunities to participate in the services. (Denver Public Library, Western History Department.)

In 1894, before the eastern syndicate purchased Baron Von Winckler's land and opened it for development, a small frame school stood at Eighteenth and Forest Streets. A two-story masonry building replaced it in 1901, and a three-story Spanish Revival–style addition followed in 1912. The Park Hill School originally employed three teachers for more than 80 children and also provided hitching posts for the children's horses. No doubt many children had to travel miles to get to school. In 1912, a new three-story school building was added to the existing structure. This addition was covered in stucco and had a red-tiled roof and Spanish-styled central parapets. Later additions included a gymnasium and an auditorium, and in 1969, a kindergarten wing and finally a cafeteria were added. This still-active school was given a Denver Landmark designation in 1994. (Above, Denver Public Library, Western History Department; below, Rebecca Dorward Collection.)

Colorado Women's College was conceived as a "Vassar of the West" by its founder, the Reverend Robert Cameron, the pastor of the First Baptist Church of Denver. The college was incorporated in 1888, though it did not open its doors until 1909. Located in northeast Denver, the school changed its name in 1967 to Temple Buell College after a Denver philanthropist who had announced plans to endow the school with a $25 million gift. However, before the gift could be realized, debts increased, and enrollment fell. In 1973, the institution was renamed Colorado Women's College, and in 1982, it merged with the University of Denver. Now, this 26-acre campus houses the Johnson and Wales University, offering programs to train chefs, culinary professionals, food media, and restaurant architects and designers. (Above, Denver Public Library, Western History Department; below, *Denver Municipal Facts*, 1914, Denver Public Library Western History Department.)

The Park Hill Branch Library was built in 1920 as one of the many Carnegie Foundation libraries across the country. It was designed in the Spanish Renaissance Revival style by well-known architect brothers Merrill H. and Burnham Hoyt. The single story with basement structure stands at 4703 Montview Boulevard. Inside the main reading room, visitors find the old-time flavor of a cast-stone fireplace, beamed ceiling, diamond-paned windows, window seats, and built-in bookcases. It is a real treasure. (Above, Denver Public Library, Western History Department; below, Rebecca Dorward Collection.)

With the beginning of the Great Depression in 1929, residential construction in Park Hill nearly stopped as the economy turned sour, aided perhaps by the serious dustbowl conditions in farming regions. In 1933, one in every four Coloradans was out of work. Charities became overburdened with requests. Many self-help groups developed, such as the Unemployed Citizens League in 1932, founded by unemployed architect Charles Dinwoody Strong. This group was able to find odd jobs to do for food or clothing. Slowly the Depression eased but not without a new awareness of the needs of the poor. This view is of present-day Seventeenth Avenue Parkway looking east. (Rebecca Dorward Collection.)

From 1930 to 1932, only two Tudor Revival–style houses were permitted, but completions were slow. In fact, along Montview Boulevard, only one residence was permitted in the early 1930s, the all-brick Tudor Revival–style house at 4343 Montview Boulevard in 1934. By that time, the majority of lots in Park Hill had been purchased and built up, and only infill properties remained. The Montview Boulevard Presbyterian Church is still an active part of the Park Hill community. This recent photograph (below) shows the older additions, with snow on the ground. (Both, Rebecca Dorward Collection.)

Seven

POSTWAR GROWING PAINS

When America entered World War II in 1941, the changes across the county included women filling traditional male jobs, a halt to residential construction, and a scarcity of consumer goods. A housing shortage occurred after the war ended, when GIs returned, leading to a residential building boom of no-frills, quickly completed houses. This new minimal traditional style met the high demand. New federal laws against segregation, followed by times of civil unrest, were felt even in Park Hill. In Denver, some black families moved from traditional neighborhoods closer to downtown, looking to buy in Park Hill and other suburban areas. The existing mostly white suburban owners responded by moving out, as "white flight" here and in other urban U.S. cities. To mitigate unrest and keep Park Hill the finest residential area in Denver, residents and clerics formed the Park Hill Action Committee in 1960 with assistance from the Montview Presbyterian, Blessed Sacrament Catholic, Park Hill Christian, Park Hill Baptist, Park Hill Congregational, Park Hill Methodist, and St. Thomas Episcopal Churches. Meetings with real estate brokers, politicians, and other residents were intended to stop "white flight" and achieve balanced integration. The group succeeded a year later in slowing the panic selling of real estate, tightening zoning ordinances to end violations, and increasing community awareness of cogent issues. Conflict ensued with the Denver Public School Board, which opposed mandatory busing, leading to the 1968 Noel resolution, designed to promote integrated schools. This resolution was later rescinded, leading to a lawsuit filed by eight Park Hill families. The Keyes case of the early 1970s went to the U.S. Supreme Court and brought national attention to Park Hill. The court ruled that school busing to achieve integration was required, which led to years of racial unrest in Denver. But few neighborhoods in the country were as expressly open to voluntary integration concerns as was Park Hill. Dr. Martin Luther King Jr. made trips to Denver and was widely welcomed in Park Hill. After his death in 1968, Thirty-second Avenue was renamed Martin Luther King Jr. Boulevard in his memory.

In 1960, the Park Hill Action Committee (PHAC) was formed to address zoning issues and cultural unrest. Several churches and concerned citizens joined in. The original 1960 officers of the Park Hill Action Committee are (standing) Jim Gilbert, treasurer; and Joe Schmitz, vice-chairman; (seated) Mrs. Kenneth Whiting, secretary and block organizer; and Ed Lupberger, chairman. (Denver University Penrose Library Special Archives.)

The members of the Park Hill Action Committee became involved in community affairs. In 1962, the prestigious Cosmopolitan Club awarded the PHAC a citation for "Meritorious Service Above and Beyond the Call of Duty." Pictured are Park Hillers Ed Lupberger, chairman; Joe Schmitz, vice-chairman; and on the left, Dr. Clarence Holmes of the Cosmopolitan Club. (Denver University Penrose Library Special Archives.)

In the 1960s, Park Hill residents took on the issue of school integration. A new elementary school named Barrett Elementary opened on Twenty-ninth Avenue in North Park Hill, an area with many black families. This had the effect of school segregation, with whites attending Park Hill and blacks attending Barrett. Many parents became dissatisfied with the quality of education at Barrett. One parent, Rachel Noel, was moved to action by the removal of her daughter from Park Hill and placement at Barrett. Noel ran for the Denver School Board and, in 1965, became the board's first black member. She formulated a plan for the schools, known as the Noel resolution, which involved mandatory and voluntary busing to achieve racial integration. In 1969, the Noel resolution was abandoned, but the legal problems continued. (Denver University Penrose Library Special Archives.)

One of the first acts of civil unrest occurred in June 1969 against one of the Park Hill Action committee members, Art Branscombe, a journalist for the *Denver Post*. A gasoline-filled bottle with a lit fuse was thrown onto his front porch. Fortunately, the fuse did not light, and no one was hurt. The attacker was never found. This image shows Art Branscombe holding the incendiary device. Art and his wife, Bea, were active in the drive to welcome blacks into the community, and they raised their family of three girls in Park Hill. (Art and Carla Branscombe Collection.)

The Denver Public School System was sued by eight African Americans, including a man named Wilfred C. Keyes. Lawsuit followed lawsuit until the case finally made national attention by being heard by the U.S. Supreme Court. In 1973, the court ruled against the Denver Public School System, requiring a rearrangement of school boundaries and mandatory busing under court supervision. (Denver University Penrose Library Special Archives.)

The years of legal issues created unrest in Park Hill. A district court judge's house was bombed. A bomb was thrown into Wilfred C. Keyes's home. School buses were destroyed. The school district headquarters was damaged. A gunshot was fired into the office of school employee Evy Dennis. School integration was not easy to achieve anywhere in the country, and that included Park Hill. (Denver University Penrose Library Special Archives.)

On the northeast edge of the Park Hill neighborhood near Stapleton International Airport, developers wished to demolish smaller houses to construct shopping areas. That action, if taken, would have displaced several lower-income families who were happy in their homes. This led to more unrest and picketing of the area. (Denver University Penrose Library Special Archives.)

Dr. Martin Luther King Jr. made several visits to Denver in the 1960s to support the integration issues and to push for an end to the Vietnam War. He gave a speech to Park Hillers and others at the Montview Presbyterian Church in May 1967. (Denver University Penrose Library Special Archives.)

This photograph was taken at a community meeting during one of Dr. King's visits to the Denver–Park Hill area in 1967. Although always a leader in fostering civil rights, Dr. King had turned his attention to the Vietnam War by this time and was adamant about ending the conflict. Years later, after his death, a major east-west thoroughfare in Park Hill was renamed Martin Luther King Jr. Boulevard. (Denver University Penrose Library Special Archives.)

In 2002, Park Hill resident Jo Mosby received the Dr. J. Carlton Babbs Community Service Award for her activism in community and women's issues. She became the chair of the Greater Park Hill Community, Inc., (GPHC) at that time. Art Branscombe also received the Babbs Award and served on the GPHC. The award is named for the former pastor of the Park Hill United Methodist Church, J. Carlton Babbs, who played a vital role in desegregation and community improvement in Park Hill. (*Greater Park Hill News*, December 18, 2002.)

Art and Bea Branscombe received many awards for their community awareness and human relations work in Park Hill. One of their efforts, through the Park Hill Action Committee, was to provide speakers to other Denver churches to relate how to positively effect integration in schools and neighborhoods. According to Art, once other neighborhoods understood the steps taken in Park Hill to welcome families of all races, they also seemed willing to work on the problems. This award was from the State of Colorado in 1984. (Art and Carla Branscombe Collection.)

Another issue that has bothered residents for many years was the overhead airplane noise from the Denver Municipal Airport (the renamed Stapleton International Airport). Though not a serious problem until the jet age, by the 1960s, jets flew over the neighborhood often. Complaints from residents were met with promises to change the traffic patterns, which did not happen, and promises of new runways, which did not help the high level of overhead noise. (Denver University Penrose Library Special Archives, 1970s.)

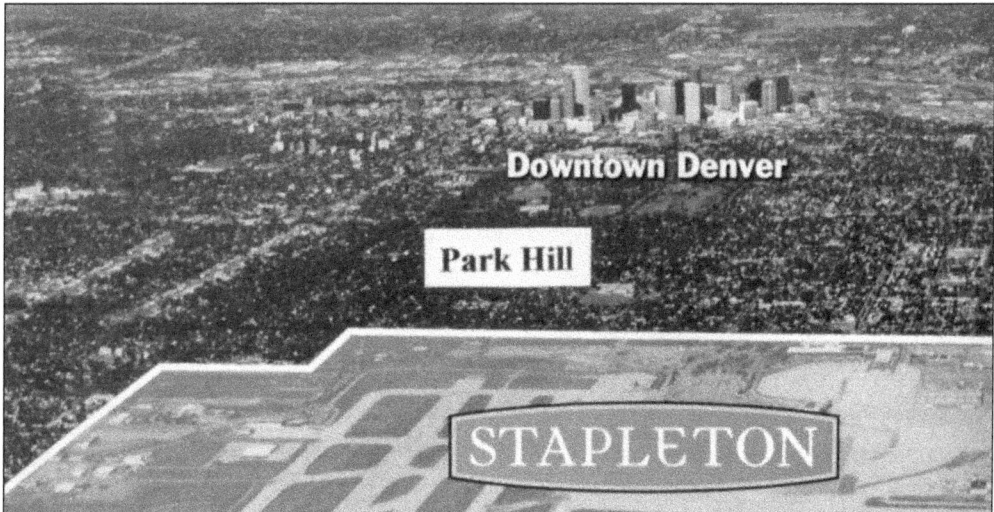

Stapleton International Airport finally closed in 1995 as the new Denver International Airport opened well east of town. Only the sleek control tower remains of the airport today. The airport land has been redeveloped into the Stapleton neighborhood, containing residences, shops, and schools. The Park Hill neighborhood became a quiet, prestigious residential area in 1995. (Stapleton Foundation.)

The Stapleton Foundation for sustainable urban communities (formerly the Stapleton Redevelopment Foundation) was established in 1990 to develop a visionary plan for the redevelopment of the Stapleton International Airport that would maximize the long-term benefit of the site. In 1995, the Stapleton Foundation published the Stapleton Master Development Plan, commonly known as the Green Book. More than 10 years later, the master development plan is still considered a visionary model of how cities can break the pattern of urban sprawl. (Stapleton Foundation.)

In 1972, two new houses were permitted on infill lots on Cherry Street, possibly the only frame residences constructed in Park Hill. By the 1990s, few vacant lots remained. A brick Colonial Revival–style residence on Ash Street was constructed, and other houses were remodeled. In most cases, homeowners constructed additions that matched the size and character of other neighborhood houses. These photographs showcase large additions to smaller existing structures. (Both, Rebecca Dorward Collection)

This block of small Tudor Revival–style homes is nestled along a snow-covered street in Park Hill. Above-average snowfalls blanketed the Front Range in the early winter of 2009. This styling became popular in the 1920s as an alternative to the ever-present bungalow of the time. They could be constructed on a single lot and usually contained two bedrooms and one bath, plus a full basement. In the basement was typically found a large boiler for central heat. (Rebecca Dorward Collection.)

Eight

PARK HILL
IN THE NEW CENTURY

The overhead noise is now gone; the civil unrest has given way to community involvement. The Park Hill neighborhood has become a wonderfully picturesque residential suburb, where the structural diversity is mirrored in the population's diversity. Some locations feature small, affordable two-bedroom homes. Other locations showcase beautiful architect-designed homes along landscaped parkways. Illustrating this prestige, Park Hill has received two honors in recent years. In 2004, the original Park Hill Addition platted by Baron von Winckler was listed as a historic district on the National Register of Historic Places, according to historian Rebecca Dorward. The national register includes the most historically significant districts in the country. In 2008, Park Hill was named in the "Top Ten Best Places to Live" by the American Planning Association.

As a tool for assisting issues of cultural diversity, the National Neighbors Conference played a role in community awareness. The nationwide conference was hosted by the Greater Park Hill Community, Inc., in 1979 and offered workshops on fair housing, school integration, and minority issues. This image shows an architect-designed home with mature landscaping. (Rebecca Dorward Collection.)

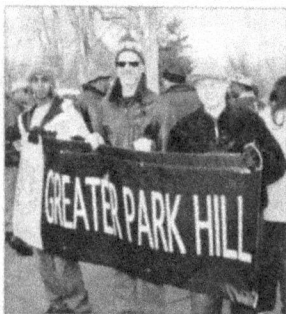

GREATER PARK HILL
COMMUNITY, INC.

Membership Information

2821 Fairfax St., Denver 80207
Phone: 303 388 0918
Fax: 303 388 0970

The Greater Park Hill Community, Inc., (GPHC) is a nonprofit neighborhood organization formed in 1960. The GPHC, managed and staffed largely by volunteers, serves as a liaison between local residents and businesses, and the City and County of Denver. This organization publishes a monthly newspaper, the *Greater Park Hill News*, which is distributed free to residents of Park Hill's administrative neighborhoods and nearby businesses. It operates a food bank and Youth Jobs Program to help young people ages 12 to 15 find summer jobs. And it sponsors an annual home tour in the fall, which has been held for the past 30 years. (GPHC brochure, 2009.)

This model of community possibilities and results began sponsoring the Greater Park Hill Home Tour in 1979. The first tour featured eight beautiful houses, plus a revitalized children's park. The newsletter article coaxed, "the Broncos are out-of-town the day of the tour . . . and hospitable hostesses well-informed with up-to-date Bronco scores just so you can enjoy the tour." The beautiful Tudor house at 6225 East Seventeenth Avenue was featured on that tour. Each year, another group of distinctive homes is featured. (GPHC newsletter, September 1979.)

Over the years, the GPHC has sponsored block parties, garden parties, and home tours, and it also operates a food bank. It truly is a model of what a community organization can be. This drawing features a home on the Greater Park Hill Home Tour from September 2009. (GPHC newsletter, September 2009.)

Denver mayor John Hickenlooper, his wife, Helen Thorpe, and son, Teddy, have lived in Park Hill for several years. A former geologist, Mayor Hickenlooper appreciates the historic houses in the neighborhood and also the short commute to his office at the City and County Building in Denver. (Denver mayor's office, 2009.)

Marcia Johnson has worked in Denver's City Council for several years. Before that, she was active in the Greater Park Hill Community, Inc. As a longtime resident of Park Hill, Johnson has been a force for community improvement. She worked for voluntary school busing and was part of the Park Hill delegation that went to Washington, D.C., for the U.S. Supreme Court case. (Courtesy Marcia Johnson.)

120

Basketball star Chauncey Billups was raised in Park Hill and attended George Washington High School. He found success in the sport of basketball at the University of Colorado. After playing two years of college basketball, he played for the NBA's Boston Celtics, Toronto Raptors, Minnesota Timberwolves, and Detroit Pistons. He was traded to the Denver Nuggets in 2008. He is married with three girls. Chauncey thinks highly of Park Hill and has the neighborhood's name tattooed on his arm. (NBA's Denver Nuggets.)

Mayor Wellington Webb was Denver's first black mayor. Though he did not live in Park Hill, as mayor he worked tirelessly for community relations throughout Denver. With him on the doorstep of the City and County Building stands history professor Thomas J. Noel (right), addressing a class of history students. (Rebecca Dorward Collection.)

The 100-year-old original Park Hill Addition was listed on the National Register of Historic Places in 2004. The addition is historically significant for community planning and development. One of the first exclusively residential areas near Denver, and one of Denver's first streetcar suburbs, this neighborhood provides a continuous record of early-20th-century residential development. Perhaps more importantly, within the Park Hill community is the story of cultural diversity and acceptance that is a model for the entire nation. (Rebecca Dorward Collection.)

This lovely Tudor Revival–style home was featured on the Greater Park Hill Home Tour in September 2002. The home tour has been a major fund-raiser for the Greater Park Hill Community since 1978. Another fund-raiser is the annual garden tour, held in the spring or early summer. The garden tour was the first fund-raiser to showcase Park Hill, and many of the Park Hill Action Committee members were involved in those tours. (*Greater Park Hill News*, September 2002.)

In 1993, Park Hill residents Cyndi Kahn, Jessica Pearson, Cathy Manchester, and others began an intensive learning program for at-risk elementary students called Summer Scholars. The Summer Scholars Program has been highly successful in improving literacy; it includes the Summer Literacy and Recreation Program, Scholars after School, and Family Literacy. This photograph shows Cyndi Kahn with Ivan Tee, the 2008 Cyndi's Scholar Award winner for achievement. (Summer Scholars, Anne Byrne, executive director, 2010.)

Another small shopping center is located on Dahlia Street and has gained in popularity in the past few years. It had formerly been a rundown shopping area with a higher-than-average crime rate. In 2005, Parkhill Community, Inc., a local nonprofit, was selected to receive a $200,000 EPA Brownfields Cleanup grant. Parkhill Community, Inc., targeted the rundown Dahlia Shopping Center and adjacent residential properties in the Northeast Parkhill neighborhood. In April 2005, the property was purchased by Parkhill Community, Inc., which will direct and oversee the cleanup under a contract with Denver Urban Renewal Authority (DURA). Cleanup of the Dahlia Square Shopping Center site will allow the community to proceed with its plans to sell the property for redevelopment. Currently the shops are experiencing solid business. (Rebecca Dorward Collection.)

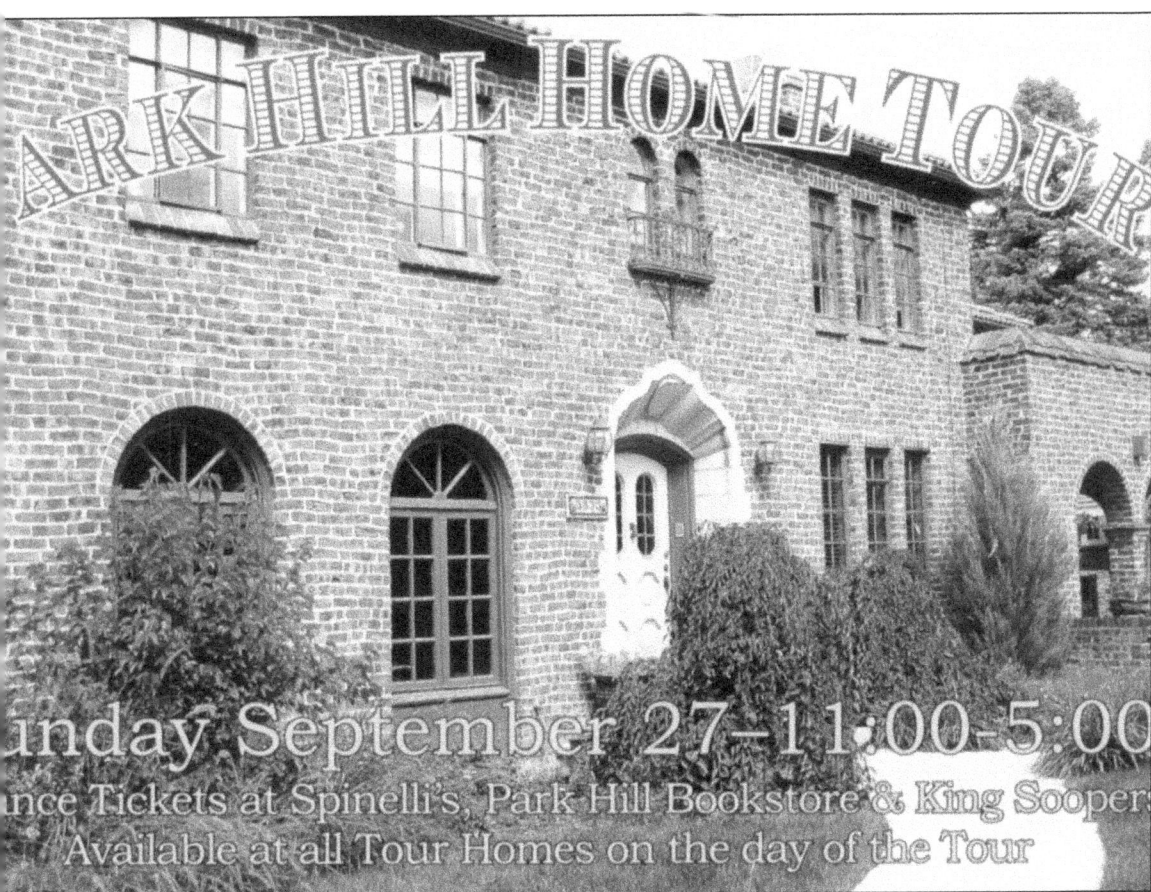

PARK HILL HOME TOUR

Sunday September 27–11:00–5:00

Advance Tickets at Spinelli's, Park Hill Bookstore & King Soopers
Available at all Tour Homes on the day of the Tour

Long-standing community efforts include maintaining a food bank and the Gathering Place, a daytime shelter. This community richly deserves the award as one of the "Top Ten Best Places to Live" by the American Planning Association. (Greater Park Hill Home Tour, 2009.)

One of Denver's premier neighborhoods, the beautiful Park Hill suburb rose for humble beginnings on the prairie outside of Denver. Today it retains a leadership role in community relations and also as one of Colorado's largest historic districts. Drive by and see for yourself. (*Denver Municipal Facts*, 1909, Denver Public Library, Western History Department.)

BIBLIOGRAPHY

Denver Municipal Facts (aka City of Denver). Denver, CO: City and County of Denver, 1908–1924.

Dorward, Rebecca C. *The Original Park Hill Historic District*. National Register of Historic Places, 2004, Colorado Historical Society, nomination and photo collection.

Grace, Stephen. *It Happened in Denver*. Morris Book Publishing, Inc., 2007.

Hunt, Geoffrey, R. *Colorado's Volunteer Infantry in the Philippine Wars*. University of New Mexico Press, 2006.

Jones, William C., and Forrest, Kenton. *Denver: A Pictorial History from Frontier Camp to Queen City of the Plains*. Boulder, CO: Pruett Publishing Company, 1973.

Leonard, Stephen J., and Noel, Thomas, J. *Denver, Mining Camp to Metropolis*, University Press of Colorado, 1990.

Noel and Norgren. *Denver: The City Beautiful, and its Architects*. 1991.

Noel, Thomas J. *Colorado Catholicism: The Archdiocese of Denver 1857-1989*. Archdiocese of Denver publication, 1989.

Noel, Thomas J., and William J. Hansen. *The Park Hill Neighborhood*. Denver, CO: Historic Denver, Inc., 2002, 2004.

Robertson, Dan, Morris Cafky, and E. J. Haley. *Denver's Street Railways: Volume 1, 1871-1900, Not An Automobile In Sight*. Denver, CO: Sundance Publications, Ltd., 1999.

PHOTOGRAPHIC COLLECTIONS

Art Branscombe photograph collections
Colorado Railroad Museum photograph collections
City councilperson Marcia Johnson collection
Denver mayor John Hickenlooper collection
Denver University, Penrose Library Special Collections
Denver Public Library, Western History Department
Denver Public School District photograph collections (and Internet Web site)
Rebecca Dorward collections
Greater Park Hill Community, Inc. collections
National Basketball Association photograph collections
Prof. Thomas J. Noel photograph collections
Summer Scholars, Anne Byrne, executive director, 2010
Stapleton Foundation brochures

Visit us at
arcadiapublishing.com